TRAUMA

How I survived it through Faith!

Dr. Robin D. Gibbs

Author

Copyright © 2020 Dr. Robin D. Gibbs

All rights reserved no part of this book shall be reproduced or transmitted in any form or by any means, electronic or mechanical, including photo copying, recording, or by any information storage or retrieval system, without permission in writing from the Author .

Dedication

This book is dedicated to those individuals who have experienced trauma through the circumstances of life that left scars or wounds that don't seem to heal. God is Able!

Acknowledgement

I would like to acknowledge my Lord and Savior, Jesus Christ, to whom all my praises flow. I would also like to thank the late Bishop Jerry Turner and my General Overseer Jennifer Turner for guiding me too Christ in this part of my life's journey. Love Always!

Table of Contents

Introduction: xiii

Chapter 1: Fatherlessness 1

Chapter 2: Insecurities 5

Chapter 3: Sexual Abuse 8

Chapter 4: Unhealthy Attachments 11

Chapter 5 Unhealthy Emotional Detachment 15

Chapter 6: Loss of Love One 17

Chapter 7: How I Am Still Standing Strong Through Faith .. 20

Introduction

A survivor can come in many different forms and from any walk of life. Being a survivor can propel one to great insight about life, especially concerning the trials they had to overcome as a survivor. As one goes through life, experiences, whether positive or negative can influence one's decision making abilities. Often times life circumstances can skew one's decisions and cause for great regret.

As a survivor of life's traumatic experiences, one must understand that life is about lessons which are meant to be learned and not disregarded. The lesson, *if learned*, will cause one to achieve above measure, excel in every caliber, and be successful in all walks of life.

Learning how I survived trauma and implemented greatness in its place is insightful to those who are experiencing or have experienced trials or hardships in their walk of life.

Trauma Definition:

According to American Psychological Association (2019), Trauma is an emotional response to a terrible event like an accident, rape or natural disaster. Immediately after the event, shock and denial are typical. Longer term reactions include unpredictable emotions, flashbacks, strained relationships and even physical symptoms like headaches or nausea.

"Trauma is the epitome of suffering in any state of being. It has lasting effects that can cause long-term emotional and physical damages and lifelong memories. It can occur in any stage of life and its effects can be very damaging to the one who is or has experienced it."
---Dr. Robin Gibbs

Dear Reader: If you'd like to view or join Bold, Intelligent, Gorgeous (B.I.G.) Girls Rock empowerment group, visit us on Facebook or website at biggirlsrock.wixsite.com/website or contact me through email at big_girlsrock@aol.com

Chapter 1

Fatherlessness

Growing up in a single parent home was very difficult as a child. There were limited resources and limited family support. My mother struggled throughout my childhood with maintaining stable shelter, food, and finances. It was very traumatic for me as a child due to the lack of necessities that were a constant issue. As a child, I watched my mother go from door to door asking for assistance. But God said in *Philippians 4:19 (KJV) 19 "But my God shall supply all your need according to his riches in glory by Christ Jesus."* Sometimes, when I was a child, this is all that I had to hold on too, believing there would be better days ahead.

Even now this scripture gets me through those days when my faith is weak. There were family members but growing up in Mobile, Alabama in a part of the city that was poverty stricken, made it hard for everyone. Assisting my mother with begging or asking around for items so we could survive was draining and discouraging as a child. Learning early on that life was about struggle and hardship was not quite the picture that I wanted to be left with at eight years old. God told me in his word.. *1 Peter 5:10*

(ERV) "Yes, you will suffer for a short time. But after that, God will make everything right. He will make you strong. He will support you and keep you from falling. He is the God who gives all grace." He chose you to share in his glory in Christ. That glory will continue forever. I would say he did just that but I recognized it later rather than sooner.

Knowing that struggling was part of my everyday life became a norm for me. I never expected anything more than struggle and hardship. That is why this scripture rings out to me today...*Deuteronomy 31:6 KJV) Be strong and of a good courage, fear not, nor be afraid of them: for the Lord thy God, he it is that doth go with thee; he will not fail thee, nor forsake thee.*

Many nights crying and hurting with so many questions. The questions were: Why is my life so hard? Why is my mother unable to care for us without the assistance of others? Why are moving so much from one family members house to the next? Why I had to go to school with hammy downs or clothes that were old? Why I can't have a normal life like all the other kids? These questions went on for years until they were drowned out by other life traumatic experiences that I experienced as a child. But this scripture set the tone for those moments ...*1 Corinthians 1:9 (AMP) God is faithful [He is reliable, trustworthy and ever true to His promise—He can be depended on], and through Him you were called into fellowship with His Son, Jesus Christ our Lord.*

Attending church as a child with family members played a major role in the light or hope that existed inside by teaching God's word. *John 14:6 (ERV) 6 Jesus answered, "I am the way, the truth, and the life. The only way to the Father is through me.* I began to think that there just may be a better life after all. My mother sent me with family members, but she rarely attended herself. One day while attending a Primitive Baptist Church, the children's choir sung ...*Jesus loves me this I know for the bible tell me so; little ones to him belong; They are weak but he is strong....*I began to replay that song in my mind over and over. It assisted me with getting through the longing for a father figure in my life. One day a ray of light came through my window and I was reminded about vacation bible school which taught us that God loves us and is always there for us. *1 John 4:19 (ERV) We love because God first loved us.* This scripture allowed me to move past the emotions of hurt and disappointment as a child growing up in a single parent home without a father being present even though I didn't really understand what was happening to me.

Encouraging Scripture: Psalm 27:10 (KJV) When my father and my mother forsake me, then the Lord will take me up.

Chapter 2

Insecurities

Insecurities plagued my mind as a child. I grew up in an environment where your confidence and self-esteem were being attacked daily by the tormenting and damaging words that were spoken over your life by parents, family, and or friends knowingly and unknowingly. Words that can influence ones outlook such as: stupid, fat, you act like your daddy, skinny, the black one, slow, special, dumb, and many other words that I have chosen not to mention. These type of words start to develop insecurities within a child. I later learned in life what God's word had to say about the matter in *Jeremiah 17:10 (NIV) "I the Lord search the heart and examine the mind, to reward each person according to their conduct, according to what their deeds deserve."*

Being a chubby kid was difficult in elementary school because children teased me. I was overweight and was heavier than all of my classmates. I remember coming home crying because the children would call me names and tease me about my weight. Today its identified as bullying and body shaming. I didn't know these words then, but I am sure the outcome is the same when someone is made to feel like they are less than a person because of the names they have been called or how they are identified within their community. One day I went home crying and upset because it was too much to handle.

The children at school didn't know what I was experiencing at home neither did the school administrators. I felt like it was way too much going on for a kid in grade school. For what it's worth, the family support at the time that I had, did the best they could with encouraging me to be strong. I was told basically to stand up for myself and don't allow anyone to pick on me "look at them and tell them the things that are wrong with them". Parents please be careful about the advice you give your children without a proper explanation. I tried this advice one time and I saw the impact it had on a child, they were now hurt by my words and that isn't what I desired. I just wanted them to leave me alone.

As I grew older, I realized that hurting others was not right, and it didn't make me feel better. I also read the word of God in *Galatians 6:7 (ESV) Do not be deceived: God is not mocked, for whatever one sows, that will he also reap.* I want to sow things that are going to produce good fruit such as: love, positivity, favor, wealth, good health, and an established relationship with God. Doing it the other way just brings chaos, trouble, horrible episodes, unforgiveness, malice, and other evil and negative

things that are not like God. So, I chose to do it God's way.

Encouraging Scripture: Psalm 139:13-14 (ESV) For you formed my inward parts; you knitted me together in my mother's womb. I praise you, for I am fearfully and wonderfully made. Wonderful are your works; my soul knows it very well.

Chapter 3

Sexual Abuse

As children we put our faith in those that we are centered around each and every day. Most of the time they are the people that our parents feel are suitable or responsible enough to be around children. Knowing and seeing parents fellowship with these individuals makes a child feel more comfortable to put their trust in those individuals that they observe and witness their parents trust. Being sexually assaulted at the age of eight by a family member was very traumatic. Then by the age of eleven I was sexually assaulted again by a family members friend child. This Scripture: *Romans 12:19 (ESV)"Beloved, never avenge yourselves, but leave it to the wrath of God, for it is written, "Vengeance is mine, I will repay, says the Lord"* rings out now more than ever because I am older and I understand God's word. Feeling as though I could not share that with anyone was very devastating. Growing up as a child was difficult because I had a hard time trusting and believing in anyone. It was like once pandoras box was opened, I had no control of my anger, resentment, or the pain that came with the hurt. Re-occurring trauma can cause one to be stuck mentally, emotionally, and sometimes physically in that event. But God said not so in *1 Corinthians 15:57 (ESV) But thanks be to God, who gives us the victory through our Lord Jesus Christ.*

Now this required me to go deeper in my relationship with God because I come to realize superficial is just that superficial. I desired a deeper relationship because the hurt was still there, and the pain would shoot through like a damaged nerve that overtime if unattended can lead to something more severe. *Proverbs 3:5-6 (NIV) says… Trust in the Lord with all your heart and lean not on your own understanding; in all your ways submit to him, and he will make your paths straight.*

Having a deeper relationship with God allowed me to understand why God allowed me to overcome these obstacles so He could get the glory out of my life. Did it matter whether I wasn't around the perpetrator anymore, or I didn't have to come face-to-face with them because I was an adult now? Yes, because healing needed to take place. This scripture helped heal the darkest moments of my memories… *Ephesians 4:31-32 (NIV) Get rid of all bitterness, rage and anger, brawling and slander, along with every form of malice. Be kind and compassionate to one another, forgiving each other, just as in Christ God forgave you.* What mattered was my true deliverance that caused me to walk in my truth so I could be a help to someone that may have experienced similar hurt.

Allowing God to come and heal my heart and remove the pain caused me to see the greater good that he was doing in my life. God will come and heal and set free that which have you bound. It's truly a blessing knowing that I don't have to walk in guilt and shame over something I really had no control over as a child. This prompts me to say…..it's okay! God knows the deepest darkest places that we have been and experienced in this life and he is here as a guiding light to lead you to the life that he has promised you. The scripture says in *Ephesians 3:20 (GNT) "To him who by means of his power working in us is able to do so much more than we can ever ask for, or even think of."*

Encouraging Scripture: Romans 5:1-6 (ESV) Therefore, since we have been justified by faith, we have peace with God through our Lord Jesus Christ. Through him we have also obtained access by faith into this grace in which we stand, and we rejoice in hope of the glory of God. Not only that, but we rejoice in our sufferings, knowing that suffering produces endurance, and endurance produces character, and character produces hope, and hope does not put us to shame, because God's love has been poured into our hearts through the Holy Spirit who has been given to us.

Chapter 4

Unhealthy Attachments

Growing up feeling alone can impacts one ability to build healthy attachments. As a child, having people around was a normal thing but I still always felt alone. I now understand what the scripture means in *Deuteronomy 31:8 (ERV)* which says *"The Lord will lead you. He himself is with you. He will not fail you or leave you. Don't worry. Don't be afraid!"*

As a child, adolescent, teenager, and or sometimes as an adult you still feel like there is no one that understands the hurt or pain that you may be experiencing. I had a hard time trusting anyone, or I didn't have anyone that I believed in to trust. These types of issues will cause one to develop unhealthy attachments to individuals or things that are harmful. When this occurs the probability of trauma is great because the relationship is fueled by lies, deceit, manipulation, which ultimately leads to abuse.

I had developed several friendship relationships with individuals over the course of high school to young adult life 'college years'. These friendships were degrading in nature because I was always the one that had to assist with finances, transportation, or room and board. This had become the norm because I realized early on that life must be like this "get while you can". It wasn't until I allowed the lord to come into my heart that I started to see things clearer. This scripture allowed me to see that I needed Christ as my friend to direct me to those who were likeminded. *John 15:14 (GNT) And you are my friends if you do what I command you.* He began to allow me to see how the relationships that I thought I was gaining was really destroying me because the attachments were unhealthy. He let me in on the secret... "as long as the enemy has you believing that you are winning, when you are losing without me *(Jesus)*, you are his". I started to evaluate the friendships that I thought was profitable for me. I was living in darkness and was blinded to the tricks of the enemy.

Scripture says in *2 Corinthians 4:4 (AMP) "among them the god of this world [Satan] has blinded the minds of the unbelieving to prevent them from seeing the illuminating light of the gospel of the glory of Christ, who is the image of God."* The scales were being removed off my eyes to see people for who they really were and see myself for who I really was as well. I knew that the friendships were superficial, but it didn't matter because I had people to party with, hang out with, go on road trips with, and just chill with. But the damage was being done behind the scenes spiritually. The enemy thought that he could influence me to do what I saw in my environment and act how I saw others did in my environment. But God said not so in *Genesis 50:20 (ERV) It is true that you planned to do something bad to me. But really, God was planning good things. God's plan was to use me to save the lives of many pe*ople. And that is what happened.

When I started to realize who he was then I began to rejoice. *Psalm 136:3 (ERV) Praise the Lord of lords! His faithful love will last forever.* Then I started to realize who I was in him. *Galatians 3:26 (KJV)informed me that.. "For ye are all the children of God by faith in Christ Jesus."* My outlook on life started to change. I started to change. The choices I made started to change and I desired change because he showed me in his word that it was possible. *Matthew 5:6 (ERV) Great blessings belong to those who want to do right more than anything else. God will fully satisfy them.* God began to show me all the danger he kept me from when I was blind and under the influence of the enemy and his illusions. The first lesson I had to learn was to fall in love with Jesus then I had to learn to fall in love with me.

Encouraging Scripture: Zephaniah 3:17 (ERV) The Lord your God is with you. He is like a powerful soldier. He will save you. He will show how much he loves you and how happy he is with you. He will laugh and be happy about you.

Chapter 5

Unhealthy Emotional Detachment

Trauma can cause one to develop maladaptive behaviors which includes unhealthy emotional detachments. I was detached emotionally from my surroundings and caring for others, having the inability to really sympathize or empathize with others. Growing up experiencing neglect, emotional, and sexual abuse can stunt healthy emotional growth and development. But God's word states in *1 John 4:8 (TLB) "But if a person isn't loving and kind, it shows that he doesn't know God—for God is love."* I really didn't have this love because of hurt, anger, pain, unforgiveness, and the lack of joy that was inside. I was emotionally disconnected to individuals I was around and that loved me.

Experiencing unhealthy emotional detachments will try to handicap you from reaching your full potential in Christ, finding your purpose, and receiving your blessings. God spoke through his word in *2 Corinthians 13:5 (ERV) Look closely at yourselves. Test yourselves to see if you are living in the faith. Don't you realize that Christ Jesus is in you? Of course, if you fail the test, he is not in you.* I had to recognize that fear is what kept me from opening my heart and loving the way that God wanted me to love.

When I read this scripture it became more clear to me... *1 John 4:18 (TLB) We need have no fear of someone who loves us perfectly; his perfect love for us eliminates all dread of what he might do to us. If we are afraid, it is for fear of what he might do to us and shows that we are not fully convinced that he really loves us.* It gave me a clear understanding of why his love wasn't working like it should in my life. I really didn't know him.

Letting God in was the best thing that could have happened. This is when I started to experience real love, real hope, real joy, and a real peace from all those tormenting things that had manifested itself in me from childhood.

Encouraging Scripture: Psalm 136:26 (ERV) Praise the God of heaven! His faithful love will last forever.

Chapter 6

Loss of a Love One

Death can be very difficult even for some Christians. After giving my life to Christ, I started to view life and the world differently in many ways. I was becoming more grounded in my faith and my walk as a servant. Then I was shaken, and my faith was tested when my spiritual father passed away. I was angry, hurt, and disappointed. I really had to dig deep in my faith and find in *Mathew 5:4 (ERV) Great blessings belong to those who are sad now. God will comfort them.* I was being taught about death and the process of death in my ministry.

However, when I had to experience it, the surprise of being without someone that had a major influence in my making, was very traumatic. I could not understand why this had happened to someone I loved and cared about. I started to experience the process of grief immediately. However, I was unable to recognize God's hand moving the entire time. He told me in *Psalm 121:5 (KJV) "The LORD is thy keeper: the LORD is thy shade upon thy right hand."* I didn't blame God or anyone. I just felt that it was unfair and untimely. Funny right! Well I guess it would be if you always had someone that guided you in God's word, wanted the best for you, and encouraged you to live on purpose. The word was there to comfort in *Matthew 24:36 (GNT) No one knows, however, when that day and hour will come— neither the angels in heaven nor the Son; the Father alone knows.*

This was a time in my life where I believed that I needed all key players on deck that had my best interest at heart to assist me with making the next steps on my journey in life. I heard the Lord speak to my spirit in *2 Corinthians 5:8 (CEV) "We should be cheerful, because we would rather leave these bodies and be at home with the Lord."* This calmed my spirit for that moment then the traumatic experience of the sudden death of my loved one began to creep in and set in my heart. I started to feel confused and lost. This was not because I was not being taught the word in my ministry, but it was because I NEVER experienced a loss of a love one that I genuinely loved and cared for.

Experiencing re-occurring trauma can cause one to be damaged and not even recognize it. God spoke softly to my heart in *Ecclesiastes 3:1-2 (AMP) "There is a season (a time appointed) for everything and a time for every delight and event or purpose under heaven— A time to be born and a time to die; A time to plant and a time to uproot what is planted."* This assisted me with overcoming the traumatic experience of losing a dear love one. I learned that while God place individuals in your life, they are not meant to stay for eternity but for you to give and receive love. Your faith will increase and so will your desire to love the way God wants you to love.

Encouraging Scripture: Revelation 21:4 (NIV) "He will wipe every tear from their eyes. There will be no more death or mourning or crying or pain, for the old order of things has passed away."

Chapter 7

How I Am Still Standing Strong Through Faith

At an early age, life yielded some unfortunate events that caused me to have doubt about my existence as a human being. Understanding how hurt and disappointment plagued my mind and filtered into my heart allowed me to realize that I had to do something to change the path that I had become familiar with experiencing. Faith made it doable, but God made it possible. Having to find a place in my heart to trust in something that was not tangible……*difficult but necessary.* Thinking back over how that life tried to stunt my growth, throw me off from finding my purpose, and handicapping me into believing I was forever going to be a debilitated soul… God said not so.

I learned that he made me new *once I accepted him into my life… 2 Corinthians (ERV)5:17 Therefore, if anyone is in Christ, the new creation has come: The old has gone, the new is here!* Those fears that didn't allow me to believe I was good enough dissolved. When I started to believe as long as He was with me nothing was impossible. This scripture added courage…. *Philippians 4:13 (NKJV)I can do all things through Christ who strengthens me.* Those fears became a part of my past. Those doubts that tried to discredit what God made me and who he made me to be… disappeared once I learned to trust in him. *Proverbs 3:5-6 (NIV) says… "Trust in the Lord with all your heart and lean not on your own understanding; in all your ways submit to him, and he will make your paths straight."* My path became straight and I started to see with clarity. This clarity brought me closer to God and his will for my life. It was unfamiliar territory, but I found it to be dependable, sustainable and durable. It was and is able to stand any test that rise in my life.

    Now, I'm still in the process of allowing God to allow me to overcome traumatic experiences in my life that may try to hinder his purpose in my life. I am still pressing into him allowing him to lead the way. I can't go wrong if he is in control. Faith has played a major role in allowing me to put my trust in someone that loves me more than I love myself. *John 15:13 (KJV) tells me that "Greater love hath no man than this, that a man lay down his life for his friends."* As I continue on this journey, I have come to realize that life's experiences can be traumatic, but my faith will continue to lead me to the rock of my salvation. *Psalm 62:6 (KJV) He only is my rock and my salvation: he is my defense; I shall not be moved.* I will continue to stand on His word.

Support is very important to assist one with overcoming personal trauma along with the word of God. I could not have done it by myself. The word lest us know that we need others that believe like us to cheer us on…. *Matthew 18:20 (TLB) For where two or three gather together because they are mine, I will be right there among them."* God lead me to people who had my back 100 percent. It started with my spiritual leaders who I am forever indebted to until this day. He then started to build my support system up in other areas with people of all walks of life. Words cannot express my gratitude for them pushing me, encouraging me, and seeing the best in me when I didn't see it in myself. I had and still have an awesome support system that continues to encourage and support me on this journey. Trauma was a major part of me being shaped. Why? Because I learned who to trust and who not to trust. What to believe in and what not to believe in. Remember God is still in control.

Encouraging scripture: Isaiah 40:31 (AMP) But those who wait for the Lord [who expect, look for, and hope in Him] Will gain new strength and renew their power; They will lift up their wings [and rise up close to God] like eagles [rising toward the sun]; They will run and not become weary, They will walk and not grow tired. Amen!!!

References

American Psychological Association. (2019). *Recovering emotionally from disaster*. Retrieved from https://www.apa.org/helpcenter/recovering-disasters

About the Author

Dr. Robin Gibbs is a native of Mobile, Alabama. She earned her PhD from Grand Canyon University in Phoenix, Arizona. This was achieved after earning a Master of Arts degree in Counseling from Prairie View A&M University and Bachelor of Science in Administration of Justice from Texas Southern University.

Dr. Robin Gibbs journey in life led her to inspire, encourage, and motivate others through her ministry, her career, and her way of life.

She is the founder of the group Bold, Intelligent, Gorgeous (BIG) Girls Rock which seeks to inspire those that need support. She also believes that with God and the right support, possibilities are endless.

Daily Scripture Log:

Made in the USA
Columbia, SC
13 January 2021